Sophie Ellis-Bexto

SOPHIE ELLIS-BEXTO

BIOGRAPHY

From Dancefloor Hits to New Beginnings: The Inspiring Journey of Her Musical Evolution, Personal Triumphs, and the Creative Spark Behind Her Latest Work

Gary M. Phelan

Sophie Ellis-Bexton

Copyright © 2025 by Gary M. Phelan

All Rights Reserved

No part of this work may be reproduced, distributed, or transmitted by any means, whether physical or electronic, such as photocopying, recording, or other forms of mechanical or digital reproduction, without the express written consent of the publisher.

DISCLAIMER

This book offers an independent exploration of Sophie Ellis-Bextor's life and achievements. It is not affiliated with or endorsed by any other publications about her. The aim of this work is to provide readers with a deeper understanding of her personal journey and is intended purely for informational purposes. Readers are encouraged to verify any specific details on their own. Rather than replacing existing sources, this book serves as an additional resource to enrich the overall knowledge of Sophie Ellis-Bextor's story.

TABLE OF CONTENTS

Prologue **6**

    Chapter 1 ....**12**

Who is Sophie Ellis-Bextor? **12**

    Chapter 2 ....**19**

Theaudience and the Road to Solo Stardom **19**

    Chapter 3 ....**27**

Breaking Through – The Release of Her First Solo Album **27**

    Chapter 4 ....**36**

Creative Struggles and Reinvention **36**

    Chapter 5 ....**44**

Dancing Through the Years – The Evolution of Her Music **44**

    Chapter 6 ....**53**

Personal Growth and Creative Freedom **53**

    Chapter 7 ....**62**

Facing Challenges and Finding New Paths 62

    Chapter 8 71

Behind the Scenes – Sophie Ellis-Bextor's Personal Life 71

    Chapter 9 78

Perimenopop – The Creative Spark Behind Her Latest Work 78

    Chapter 10 86

Looking Ahead – Sophie's Legacy and Continuing Impact 86

Epilogue 93

Prologue

Picture this: the lights are flashing, the beat is infectious, and the crowd is moving as one. You're on the dancefloor, surrounded by energy, swept up in the rhythm of the music. But this isn't just any night; this is the feeling Sophie Ellis-Bextor's music evokes in her listeners. She's the force behind those unforgettable hits—tracks that have become anthems of a generation. Yet, Sophie's journey is far more than just the songs she creates. It's about the ongoing evolution of an artist, a woman who's never stopped pushing forward, learning, and rediscovering herself in both her music and life.

For many of us, Sophie Ellis-Bextor represents more than just a pop sensation. Her name is synonymous with songs that defined an era—tracks like "Murder on the Dancefloor" and "Groovejet," which took over the charts and secured her place in music history. However, Sophie's story isn't solely about those iconic moments.

It's about the constant reinvention that's fueled her career and personal growth. Through the peaks and valleys of fame, Sophie has maintained a singular ability to transform her sound, refresh her identity, and keep her music as relevant today as it was when she first stepped into the limelight.

What sets Sophie apart is not just the sheer number of hits she's amassed, but her ability to reshape herself and her music over time. In an industry where trends can be fleeting, Sophie's career has been defined by her determination to remain authentic while evolving with each new chapter. She's never been content to rest on her laurels; instead, she's embraced new challenges, new creative directions, and even new life stages. Her sound has shifted, but her core—her unique voice and perspective—has remained unshaken.

Her journey is one of transformation—an artist's evolution that mirrors the experiences of anyone who has faced change, growth, or the need to redefine themselves.

It's not just about the music; it's about resilience, authenticity, and the courage to navigate life's uncertainties with grace and determination.

This biography aims to offer a closer look at Sophie's life, not just as a musician, but as a person who has continuously reinvented herself. It's a celebration of how she's embraced her craft and her life, facing challenges with an unwavering commitment to creativity. As you read through Sophie's story, you'll discover the moments that shaped her—those that pushed her to go deeper into her artistry and evolve in ways that many never thought possible. Her journey is marked by countless reinventions, each one showing her resilience and ability to stay true to herself, even in the face of obstacles.

Through her music, Sophie has always shown us the power of change—not just in her work, but in how she lives her life. With each album, each new project, she continues to explore what it means to evolve. Her journey speaks to anyone who has ever felt the need to adapt, to grow, and to remain faithful to their core self despite the pressures of the world around them. Sophie's music, both the hits and the quieter moments, tells the story of someone who is constantly learning, growing, and finding new ways to express herself. Her authenticity shines through, and that's what makes her a lasting figure in the world of music.

In this book, you will get an inside look into Sophie's world, her creative process, and the personal experiences that have shaped her into the artist we know today. We will explore her early days in the music scene, her rise to stardom, the personal and professional obstacles she's faced, and the ways in which she's continuously pushed herself to grow. It's a look at the evolution of a woman who has never been afraid to face the unknown, to challenge herself, and to embrace new ideas.

But what makes Sophie's story truly captivating is her ability to find joy in reinvention. Her journey is one of embracing change, taking risks, and staying curious. Each new phase in her life and career has been an opportunity for her to explore new creative possibilities, to experiment, and to stay true to her unique voice. It's a message that resonates far beyond the music industry—it's about life itself, about how we all have the power to reinvent ourselves, no matter where we're at in our journey.

Sophie Ellis-Bextor is more than a pop star—she's an artist who has shown us that transformation isn't something to fear, but something to embrace. Her story is about growing through the challenges, learning from the past, and moving forward with an open heart and mind. And that's what this biography captures—Sophie's enduring ability to transform herself while remaining true to the music that has always defined her. Her journey is a reminder that reinvention is not just possible, but necessary for growth, and that it's something we can all learn from.

As we explore Sophie's world, you'll gain insight into the mindset of someone who is constantly evolving, and you'll see how she's been able to carve out a path that is uniquely her own. Whether it's her struggles with fame, her efforts to maintain creative control, or her journey into new personal and professional territories, Sophie's story is one of triumph over adversity. It's a tale of an artist who has never stopped learning, never stopped evolving, and never stopped embracing the power of change. This biography is not just for Sophie's fans—it's for anyone who has ever faced the challenge of finding their true self, and who understands that transformation is the key to success, in music and in life.

Chapter 1

Who is Sophie Ellis-Bextor?

Born in Hounslow, London, on April 10, 1979, Sophie's early years were defined by her exposure to a creative world. Growing up in a household where artistic expression was highly valued, Sophie was surrounded by a wealth of cultural influences from the start. Her mother, Janet Ellis, was a television presenter, and her father, Robin Bextor, worked as a documentary filmmaker. With such a background, it was no surprise that Sophie developed a keen interest in the arts. This environment encouraged her to explore her own creativity, which, over time, would lead her to the world of music.

While Sophie's family was known for their work in television and film, music was an equally significant part of her upbringing. The Ellis-Bextor home was filled with

Sophie Ellis-Bextor

a variety of musical influences, as both of her parents were passionate about the art form. Their diverse taste in music exposed Sophie to a wide range of genres, sparking a love for melodies and rhythms that would become central to her life. Early on, Sophie found herself experimenting with sounds, playing the piano, and developing a strong desire to make music her own. For Sophie, music wasn't just an interest—it became a defining part of her identity.

Her passion for music grew steadily, although it didn't immediately translate into a career. As a teenager, Sophie initially pursued acting and attended the prestigious Sylvia Young Theatre School in London. Here, she honed her skills in performance, but it wasn't long before she realized that her true calling lay in music rather than acting. This was a significant turning point for Sophie, as she began to channel her energy into developing her musical abilities. Her love for the stage remained, but it was music that truly captured her heart.

While Sophie's decision to focus on music was a pivotal moment, her transition wasn't an immediate leap to fame. Instead, it was a gradual process of self-discovery. She began performing at smaller venues, testing her own songwriting abilities, and exploring the world of music on her own terms. This period was crucial in shaping Sophie's identity as an artist. It was during these early performances that Sophie started to find her voice—both literally and figuratively.

A significant moment in Sophie's musical journey came when she joined the indie band Theaudience in the late 1990s. The band, known for its fusion of indie rock, pop, and jazz, provided Sophie with her first major opportunity to showcase her talents. As the lead singer, Sophie quickly became known for her distinctive voice and strong stage presence. Although Theaudience never achieved widespread commercial success, the experience was invaluable for Sophie. It gave her firsthand knowledge of the music industry and allowed her to refine her musical style.

The time she spent in Theaudience was formative, and it allowed Sophie to explore her vocal range and collaborate with other musicians. Through these collaborations, she learned how to adapt her voice to different styles and genres, an experience that would later serve her well in her solo career. When Theaudience disbanded in 1999, Sophie faced a new challenge—one that would define her future. Though she had enjoyed working with the band, it was clear that she was ready to pursue her own path. Determined to forge a solo career, Sophie set out to make her mark in the music world.

Her decision to become a solo artist proved to be a wise one. In 2001, Sophie released her debut album *Read My Lips*, which introduced her to a global audience. With the single "Groovejet (If This Ain't Love)," Sophie gained instant recognition. The track became an international hit, catapulting her to fame and firmly establishing her as a rising star. Shortly after, the release of "Murder on the Dancefloor" further solidified her place in pop history, earning her widespread acclaim and recognition.

But Sophie's success wasn't simply a result of good fortune. It was the outcome of years of dedication, hard work, and a deep-rooted passion for music. Her rise to fame was a culmination of the years spent exploring her musical abilities, collaborating with others, and continuously developing her unique sound. Sophie's career has been a continuous journey of artistic growth, and each step has been a reflection of her dedication to her craft.

What stands out about Sophie's career is her ability to evolve. While many artists rest on their early successes, Sophie has consistently sought new challenges and creative avenues. She hasn't been afraid to experiment with different styles and sounds, ensuring that her music continues to feel fresh and relevant. Her ability to reinvent herself without losing the essence of who she is as an artist has been one of the driving forces behind her long-lasting success.

Sophie's journey is one of perseverance. From her early days performing in small venues to becoming an internationally recognized artist, she has faced her share of challenges. However, rather than being deterred, Sophie has used these experiences to fuel her creativity and drive. She has never been content to settle for the status quo but has continuously sought ways to evolve and stay true to herself. This unwavering commitment to her music and her personal vision has been a hallmark of her career.

Sophie's story isn't just one of musical success—it's a story of personal growth. From her early years as a child in a creative household to her rise to fame as a solo artist, Sophie's journey is defined by self-discovery, resilience, and an enduring love for music. It's a reminder that success is not something that happens overnight but is the result of years of hard work, determination, and the willingness to embrace change.

Sophie Ellis-Bextor

As Sophie's career progresses, she continues to challenge herself and explore new horizons. Her music reflects her personal growth and her evolving understanding of the world around her. Sophie Ellis-Bextor is more than just a pop artist; she is an embodiment of the power of reinvention and the importance of staying true to one's creative vision.

Chapter 2

Theaudience and the Road to Solo Stardom

Sophie Ellis-Bextor's entry into the music world didn't happen overnight. It was a gradual progression, one that began with her involvement in the indie-pop band *Theaudience* in the late 1990s. Although the band's time in the spotlight was relatively brief, it played an essential role in Sophie's development as an artist. It helped her find her voice, both literally and creatively, and set the stage for the next chapter of her career—her solo debut.

Theaudience was an eclectic mix of indie rock, pop, and jazz, capturing the sound of the late '90s with its infectious rhythms and catchy tunes. As the band's lead singer, Sophie quickly became the face of the group. Her distinctive voice, full of energy and charisma, drew attention and helped the band stand out in the crowded indie music scene. They found a loyal fanbase, and while they were well-regarded critically, *Theaudience* never quite reached the level of mainstream success that many had hoped for. Still, it was clear from the outset that Sophie had the talent and presence to go much further.

Despite their critical acclaim, *Theaudience* faced limitations in terms of commercial success. The collaborative nature of the band, while giving it a sense of unity, often resulted in creative compromises. Sophie's unique sound was often shaped by the group dynamic, and over time, she began to feel that her personal artistic vision wasn't being fully realized. The band's success depended on the collective input of all its members, which, while fostering camaraderie, also stifled Sophie's ability to explore her sound independently. This growing sense of artistic restriction eventually led to her decision to leave the band and pursue a solo career.

The decision to leave *Theaudience* wasn't one Sophie made lightly. The band had been an essential part of her life, both professionally and personally, and stepping away from it meant facing the unknown. However, Sophie understood that in order to fully express herself as an artist, she needed to venture out on her own. The creative freedom she sought could not be fully realized within the confines of a group dynamic. The idea of stepping into the limelight on her own was daunting, but it also represented a unique opportunity to shape her own musical journey.

Sophie's transition from band member to solo artist was not just a career move; it was a personal transformation. While she was confident in her abilities, the thought of leaving behind the security of a band environment to become a solo performer was a huge leap. The music industry is often daunting for newcomers, and venturing into the spotlight without the backing of a band brought with it a new set of challenges. Yet, Sophie was resolute in her desire to pursue her own sound, even if it meant navigating the pressures of doing so alone.

As she left *Theaudience* behind, Sophie entered the unknown territory of being a solo artist. The excitement of carving out her own space in the music world was tempered by the pressure to succeed independently. She had no choice but to face the challenge head-on, knowing that her success would rest entirely on her shoulders. It wasn't just about creating music—it was about defining herself as an artist. The desire to establish her own identity outside the band was strong, and Sophie was determined to show the world what she was capable of on her own.

Her debut solo album, *Read My Lips*, was the first major step in this journey. Released in 2001, it marked a clear departure from the style of *Theaudience*, embracing a more polished pop sound that was uniquely her own. The album's success was a crucial milestone in Sophie's career. The single "Groovejet (If This Ain't Love)" became an international hit, propelling Sophie into the limelight. The following single, "Murder on the Dancefloor," further solidified her position in the music industry. These songs not only resonated with audiences but also reflected Sophie's ability to take risks and push her creative boundaries.

However, the success of *Read My Lips* wasn't just about commercial hits—it was about Sophie's growth as an artist. The album showcased her range as a singer and performer, while also reflecting her evolving artistic vision. With this debut, Sophie set the stage for her future work, showing that she could create music that was both personal and appealing to a broad audience.

Despite the success, the transition to solo stardom didn't come without challenges. Sophie was now fully responsible for every aspect of her career—from songwriting and production to promotion and performance. While she had the creative freedom she had longed for, it also meant that the pressure was now entirely on her shoulders. The decision to go solo meant Sophie had to not only prove herself as a musician but also as a businesswoman, navigating the complexities of the music industry alone.

This shift also required Sophie to make a series of decisions that would define her career. Being in a band had meant collaborating with others, bouncing ideas off fellow musicians, and working as part of a team. Now, as a solo artist, Sophie was tasked with forging her own direction and maintaining complete control over her sound. It was no longer about balancing the interests of multiple band members; it was about staying true to her own artistic instincts while managing the various aspects of her career.

One of the greatest challenges Sophie faced was the expectation to live up to the success she had enjoyed as part of *Theaudience*. There was a real pressure to prove that she could achieve success on her own. Being in the public eye comes with its own set of expectations, and Sophie knew that fans, critics, and the music industry would be watching closely to see if her solo career could match the potential that had been so evident in her early years with the band.

But Sophie's move into the solo realm also provided her with the freedom to experiment and express herself more authentically. The ability to explore new sounds, take creative risks, and shape her own narrative was incredibly liberating. With *Read My Lips*, Sophie introduced a fresh, more polished pop sound that allowed her to stand out from her peers. It wasn't just about catchy hooks—it was about showing the world that Sophie Ellis-Bextor had something unique to offer.

The shift from band member to solo artist also forced Sophie to reconsider her artistic identity. In *Theaudience*, she was part of a collective voice. As a solo performer, Sophie had to find her own path. She began to realize that she had a distinct sound and style that set her apart. Her solo work was a reflection of her individuality, her creative vision, and her desire to explore music in a way that felt true to herself.

Looking back on her time with *Theaudience*, it's clear that the band was a crucial step in Sophie's career. It provided her with the foundation she needed to launch her solo career, giving her experience in performing, collaborating, and navigating the music industry. However, it was her decision to step away from the band that truly allowed her to grow as an artist. While leaving *Theaudience* was a bold move, it was necessary for Sophie to fully realize her potential as a solo performer.

Today, Sophie Ellis-Bextor is known not just for her hits but for her ability to reinvent herself as an artist. The transition from *Theaudience* to solo stardom wasn't easy, but it was a pivotal moment that defined the direction of her career. The challenges she faced in going solo only helped shape her into the artist she is today. Her time with *Theaudience* gave her the tools and the experience she needed, but it was her decision to embrace the solo spotlight that allowed her to truly flourish.

Chapter 3

Breaking Through – The Release of Her First Solo Album

Sophie Ellis-Bextor's journey as a solo artist began in earnest with the release of *Read My Lips* in 2001. This debut album didn't just mark the start of her solo career; it set the stage for everything that followed, proving that she was not only capable of making an impact on the music scene but that she had the potential to define her own musical path. With this album, Sophie made it clear that she was not just another former band member but an artist in her own right, ready to claim her place in the spotlight.

The creation of *Read My Lips* was a deeply personal process for Sophie, one that allowed her to explore her artistic vision without the constraints of a band dynamic. After her time with *Theaudience*, Sophie had the freedom to express herself more openly, choosing the direction of her music with full creative control. This newfound freedom came with its challenges, of course. Without the collaborative environment of a group, Sophie was solely responsible for crafting the sound and style of her music. Yet, it was this very challenge that spurred her to produce an album that was both polished and uniquely hers.

The album blends elements of dance, pop, and electronic music with Sophie's sultry, distinct vocals, resulting in a sound that was fresh, yet familiar. The production was sleek, with sharp beats and catchy melodies that would come to define her style. Sophie knew she wanted *Read My Lips* to showcase her versatility as an artist. The music is both accessible and nuanced, a reflection of her ability to balance mainstream appeal with the desire to stay true to her own voice.

The standout moment on the album came with the release of "Groovejet (If This Ain't Love)," a track that would become a massive hit and a key moment in Sophie's career. Co-written with Italian DJ Spiller, the song became an instant classic with its infectious melody and irresistible rhythm. It was an anthem of the time, and its success didn't just cement Sophie's place in pop music—it set the tone for her future in the industry. The song's global success propelled Sophie into the spotlight, marking the moment when it was clear that she had the ability to succeed as a solo artist.

"Groovejet" reached the top of the charts in the UK and several other countries, and it was the perfect introduction to Sophie's musical talents. The track was both an expression of her unique style and a nod to the influences that had shaped her music. Its success was a sign of things to come, but it was also a demonstration of Sophie's ability to carve out her own niche in a crowded music landscape.

Following "Groovejet," Sophie's next single, "Murder on the Dancefloor," further solidified her place as a pop star. Released in late 2001, the track became one of her most well-known songs. Its catchy, upbeat tune and clever lyrics about taking control of the dancefloor resonated with audiences around the world. "Murder on the Dancefloor" wasn't just a pop hit; it was a declaration of Sophie's confidence as an artist. The song's success proved that Sophie could not only make music that people wanted to dance to but also create songs that were full of personality and depth.

The success of both "Groovejet" and "Murder on the Dancefloor" was significant not just because they were chart-topping hits, but because they allowed Sophie to establish her identity as a solo artist. She wasn't merely replicating the success she'd experienced with *Theaudience*; she was building something entirely new. *Read My Lips* was a reflection of Sophie's personal growth as an artist, one that allowed her to take risks, experiment with different sounds, and still stay true to her core.

However, with the success of her debut album came the pressure of early fame. Sophie found herself at the center of public attention, and with that came expectations. The music industry, along with her fans and critics, were now closely watching her every move. There was the expectation that Sophie would not only continue to produce hits but that she would also maintain the level of success she had achieved with her debut album. For many artists, the early years of fame can be overwhelming, and for Sophie, it was no different.

The pressure to live up to the success of *Read My Lips* was immense. There was no longer the security of being part of a band where responsibilities were shared. Sophie had to bear the weight of her success alone, navigating the ups and downs of the music industry while trying to stay grounded. The spotlight that came with her newfound fame also meant she had to contend with the pressures of maintaining her public image and keeping the momentum of her career going.

Sophie, however, remained determined not to let the pressures of fame define her. She was aware that her success in the music industry was fragile and could easily fade. Sophie knew that in order to sustain her career, she would need to continue evolving as an artist, pushing herself creatively and not resting on her past achievements. She didn't want to be just another pop star who had a moment of fame and then faded into obscurity. Sophie was committed to staying true to herself as an artist and not allowing external pressures to dictate her creative choices.

The success of *Read My Lips* was a major milestone in Sophie's career, but it also marked the beginning of a new chapter—a chapter in which she would continue to navigate the challenges of fame while also staying true to her artistic vision. The album's success set the foundation for her to grow as an artist, experiment with new sounds, and build a body of work that was uniquely her own. The songs from *Read My Lips* would remain some of her most beloved, but they also paved the way for her to explore different musical territories in the years that followed.

As the success of her debut album continued, Sophie found herself not only facing the pressures of the industry but also dealing with the personal challenges that come with fame. The spotlight had shifted entirely to her, and with that came a new level of scrutiny. Sophie learned to manage the ups and downs of her career, recognizing that with every success came the potential for both positive and negative attention. It was a delicate balance—one that required her to stay focused on her music while also learning to handle the external pressures that came with being a successful solo artist.

Sophie's ability to stay true to herself and continue evolving as an artist was key to her long-term success. She was never content to simply replicate the success of her debut album or rest on the laurels of her early hits. Instead,

Sophie used *Read My Lips* as a springboard to explore new musical directions, experiment with different sounds, and challenge herself creatively. The success of "Groovejet" and "Murder on the Dancefloor" was just the beginning of what would become a long and successful career. Sophie's ability to grow as an artist, while staying grounded in her authenticity, would define her path in the years that followed.

Looking back, *Read My Lips* was not just a debut album—it was the foundation upon which Sophie Ellis-Bextor built her career. The album marked the moment when she fully stepped into the role of a solo artist, unafraid to take risks, explore new musical landscapes, and create a sound that was entirely her own. The success of "Groovejet" and "Murder on the Dancefloor" showed the world that Sophie had something special to offer. Her debut album was not just a commercial success; it was a statement of her potential as an artist. It was the start of an extraordinary journey—one that would see Sophie evolve into one of the most respected figures in pop music.

The journey that began with *Read My Lips* was one of constant growth, change, and reinvention. As Sophie moved forward in her career, she continued to build on the foundation established by her debut album. Her ability to remain true to herself while adapting to the ever-changing landscape of the music industry would become the hallmark of her career. *Read My Lips* wasn't just the beginning of Sophie's success—it was the moment that defined her as an artist and set the stage for everything that followed.

Chapter 4

Creative Struggles and Reinvention

After the breakout success of *Read My Lips*, Sophie found herself at a critical juncture. She had made a substantial impact on the music scene, but the true test of her longevity was how she would evolve in the face of commercial expectations. The success of her debut album, driven by hits like "Groovejet (If This Ain't Love)" and "Murder on the Dancefloor," meant that Sophie was no longer an emerging talent—she was now an established artist with a fanbase and a significant public profile. This brought with it a set of challenges that went beyond simply creating good music. Sophie had to navigate the pressures of maintaining her place in a constantly shifting industry, all while ensuring that her music stayed true to her personal voice.

The central struggle for Sophie during this period was how to reconcile the pressures of the commercial music industry with her desire for artistic freedom. The music industry often places high demands on artists to follow trends, produce music that appeals to a broad audience, and replicate the success of past hits. This can lead to a sense of creative confinement, where the desire for commercial success overshadows personal artistic growth. For Sophie, the challenge was not just about producing music that would sell but finding ways to remain true to her artistic identity and continue developing as a musician.

Shooting from the Hip, her second album released in 2003, reflected this internal conflict. Sophie wanted to explore a broader musical range, but she was also aware that she needed to stay within the bounds of pop music's expectations. This tension between wanting to innovate and the pressure to deliver more of the same pop hits was a key theme in her creative process. *Shooting from the Hip* featured a more experimental sound than *Read My Lips*, incorporating elements of rock, jazz, and soul. It was clear that Sophie was attempting to break free from the strict pop mold, yet the album still carried enough commercial appeal to keep her connected to her mainstream audience.

While *Shooting from the Hip* was an album that saw Sophie take risks, the response was mixed. Some listeners appreciated her boldness in moving away from the purely commercial pop sound of her debut, while others missed the catchy, radio-friendly hits that had made her famous. Sophie, as a result, found herself at a crossroads. Her desire to move away from the commercial pop model was in conflict with the commercial demands of the industry. There was a growing sense that Sophie had something deeper to offer musically, but the mainstream pop world was more focused on maintaining its formulaic approach to success.

The mixed reception of *Shooting from the Hip* highlighted the struggle many artists face when attempting to evolve while still catering to their audience's expectations. Sophie's decision to experiment with different sounds was a bold move, but it came with risks. She knew that evolving as an artist meant confronting these challenges head-on, but it also required a great deal of patience and persistence. For Sophie, it was not just about making the music the industry wanted—it was about making the music that she felt was true to who she was becoming as an artist.

One of the most difficult aspects of this period was the pressure to constantly evolve while still meeting the expectations of her fans. The success of *Read My Lips* had established Sophie as a major pop figure, but that success also came with the expectation that she would continue to produce more of the same. However, Sophie was not content with simply being known for a few catchy hits. She wanted her music to reflect her growth as a person and as an artist. This desire to evolve creatively was something Sophie struggled with, especially as the industry seemed more interested in commercial success than artistic depth.

As Sophie worked on her next album, *Trip the Light Fantastic* (2007), she began to find a way to balance her artistic growth with her desire for commercial success. The album was a more polished and radio-friendly pop record compared to *Shooting from the Hip*, but it still retained the emotional depth that Sophie had developed in her previous work. This balance between creative freedom and commercial appeal was a key factor in the success of *Trip the Light Fantastic*. It allowed Sophie to connect with a broader audience while still staying true to her personal voice as an artist.

The success of *Trip the Light Fantastic* was a testament to Sophie's ability to adapt while maintaining her authenticity. The album showcased her continued evolution as an artist, but it also demonstrated her understanding of the music industry's demands. Sophie's willingness to experiment with different sounds and themes allowed her to stand out from her peers, while her ability to create music that was both personal and accessible ensured that she remained relevant in the ever-changing pop music landscape.

Throughout her career, Sophie has continued to grapple with the challenges of maintaining her artistic integrity while navigating the commercial demands of the music industry. The struggles she faced during the creation of *Shooting from the Hip* were not unique to her; many artists face similar pressures when trying to evolve in a world that values success over artistic expression. However, Sophie's ability to overcome these challenges and continue to reinvent herself has been a defining characteristic of her career. She has never been content to simply rest on her past successes, instead choosing to push the boundaries of her creativity while staying true to the themes that have always been important to her.

Sophie's creative reinvention is not just about making different music; it's about maintaining her voice in an industry that often rewards conformity. Her willingness to take risks, experiment with new sounds, and explore different themes has allowed her to stay relevant in an industry that constantly changes. While her earlier hits may have defined her career in its early stages, it is her ability to reinvent herself with each new album that has allowed Sophie to remain an important figure in the music world.

In looking at Sophie's career, it becomes clear that her journey is one of continuous self-discovery. She has faced the pressures of fame, the expectations of the music industry, and the challenges of maintaining relevance, but she has never wavered in her commitment to her art. Her creative struggles and reinventions are a testament to her resilience as an artist, and her ability to stay true to her artistic vision in the face of these struggles is what has allowed her to remain a respected and influential figure in the music industry.

Through her music, Sophie has shown that reinvention does not mean losing oneself in the process—it means finding new ways to express the same core truths. Her struggles with maintaining authenticity while navigating the changing tides of the music industry reflect the broader struggles faced by many artists. Sophie Ellis-Bextor's story is not just one of musical success—it is a story of creative perseverance and the ongoing quest for artistic freedom in an industry that often values conformity over individuality.

Chapter 5

Dancing Through the Years – The Evolution of Her Music

Sophie Ellis-Bextor's musical journey is marked by an ongoing evolution, a continuous process of reinvention that has allowed her to stay relevant in an ever-changing industry. While her debut album *Read My Lips* established her as a pop sensation with its catchy dance-pop anthems, Sophie's path has never been about staying in one place. Over the years, her sound has evolved from the high-energy pop of her early career to a more nuanced and diverse musical palette. This chapter explores Sophie's transformation, showcasing how her music has changed with time while still reflecting the essence of who she is as an artist.

Sophie Ellis-Bexton

When Sophie first entered the spotlight as a solo artist, her debut album *Read My Lips* (2001) quickly made her a household name. Songs like "Groovejet (If This Ain't Love)" and "Murder on the Dancefloor" were infectious pop hits that captured the essence of the early 2000s. The success of these tracks introduced Sophie as a dynamic force in pop music, blending catchy melodies with her signature sultry vocals. At the time, dance-pop was a dominant genre, and Sophie's style fit perfectly within it. However, despite the success of *Read My Lips*, Sophie knew that she could not simply rest on the laurels of her debut work. She was aware that in order to grow as an artist, she would need to explore new sounds and directions.

The pressure to maintain commercial success while still evolving artistically became one of Sophie's key struggles. The music industry often expects artists to deliver more of the same after a successful debut, and Sophie was no exception. With the release of her second album, *Shoot from the Hip* (2003), Sophie found herself at a crossroads. She had enjoyed the success of *Read My Lips*, but she also wanted to break free from the constraints of a pop formula. *Shoot from the Hip* was a bold move—a step into uncharted territory that explored new genres and sounds. The album featured a mix of rock, jazz, and soul influences, marking a departure from the sleek pop of her first record.

The shift in musical direction on *Shoot from the Hip* was met with mixed reactions. Some praised Sophie for taking risks and experimenting with her sound, while others felt that the album lacked the catchy hooks that had made her famous. Despite the varied reception, *Shoot from the Hip* was an important moment in Sophie's career. It demonstrated her willingness to experiment with different musical styles and themes, signaling that she was more than just a pop artist. Sophie was eager to show that she was capable of creating music with depth, and *Shoot from the Hip* marked the start of a new phase in her musical journey.

However, this experiment in musical reinvention wasn't without its challenges. Sophie faced the pressure of balancing the desire to evolve with the commercial expectations that came with her newfound fame. Her fans, many of whom had fallen in love with her dance-pop hits, were unsure how to respond to this more experimental sound. Sophie, however, was committed to her creative vision and refused to be limited by what was expected of her. She knew that in order to continue growing as an artist, she had to push boundaries and explore new creative directions.

The album *Trip the Light Fantastic* (2007) marked a return to a more mainstream pop sound, but it also incorporated the growth that Sophie had experienced in the years since *Shoot from the Hip*. *Trip the Light Fantastic* had all the elements of a pop album—catchy melodies, danceable beats—but it also retained the emotional depth and introspective qualities that Sophie had begun exploring in her previous work. The album's success was a turning point for Sophie, as it demonstrated that she could strike a balance between creative evolution and commercial appeal. Her hit single "Catch You" became a major success, reaffirming Sophie's place in the pop world while also reflecting her growth as a songwriter.

With *Trip the Light Fantastic*, Sophie proved that she could reinvent herself without losing her ability to create infectious, memorable pop songs. The album resonated with a broad audience, and it marked a return to the kind of radio-friendly hits that made her a star in the first place. However, Sophie's decision to blend her more experimental influences with pop conventions was a reflection of her desire to evolve as an artist without abandoning the core of what made her successful. The album was a perfect example of Sophie's ability to adapt to changing musical landscapes while staying true to her own voice.

In 2011, Sophie released *Make a Scene*, an album that took yet another step in her artistic evolution. This time, she embraced the world of electronic dance music, working with several prominent DJs and producers. The album's lead single, "Not Giving Up on Love," was a collaboration with Dutch DJ Armin van Buuren, and it marked a more overt shift towards EDM. With *Make a Scene*, Sophie fully immersed herself in the electronic dance scene, exploring a sound that was both modern and reflective of the global popularity of EDM at the time.

The album's electronic direction represented a significant departure from the pop sound that had defined much of Sophie's earlier work. However, it also showed her willingness to embrace new trends and experiment with different genres. While *Make a Scene* did not achieve the same level of commercial success as some of her previous albums, it was still an important part of Sophie's ongoing evolution. The album's success in the EDM world proved that Sophie was not just a pop star but an artist capable of crossing over into new territories and connecting with a different audience. *Make a Scene* was a testament to Sophie's creativity and willingness to take risks.

As Sophie continued to develop as an artist, she began to explore new genres and sounds on each of her subsequent albums. Her 2016 album *Familia* marked yet another shift in her approach to music, incorporating elements of folk, indie, and electronic influences. The album was deeply personal, exploring themes of love, family, and personal growth. The lead single, "Come with Us," showcased Sophie's ability to blend different genres while retaining the authenticity that had always defined her work.

Familia was a departure from the dance-pop sounds of her earlier albums, and it was clear that Sophie had grown as both an artist and a person. The album's introspective nature and the more organic, stripped-down sound marked a return to a more authentic version of Sophie. It was an album that reflected her life experiences, and it resonated with listeners who had grown with her over the years. Sophie's ability to transition between genres while maintaining her core identity as an artist is one of the key elements that has made her such a respected figure in the music industry.

Sophie Ellis-Bextor

Over the years, Sophie has consistently demonstrated her ability to evolve musically without losing the essence of what makes her unique. Whether exploring the world of electronic dance music, folk influences, or more introspective, personal themes, Sophie has never been afraid to step outside the boundaries of the mainstream pop world. Her willingness to experiment with different sounds and genres has allowed her to stay relevant in a rapidly changing industry, while her commitment to authenticity has ensured that her music continues to resonate with listeners.

The evolution of Sophie's music is a testament to her creative resilience. She has never been content to rest on her past successes or follow the trends of the moment. Instead, she has continually sought to push herself creatively, exploring new genres and production techniques while maintaining the core elements that have made her such a beloved artist. Sophie's ability to evolve while staying true to herself is what has allowed her to remain a relevant and influential figure in the music world, and her musical journey is one that continues to inspire.

Chapter 6

Personal Growth and Creative Freedom

When Sophie first ventured into the music world, much of the creative direction was shaped by others—producers, record labels, and the overarching expectations of the music industry. As her career developed, Sophie began to recognize the importance of having ownership over her music, and the desire to shape her own artistic destiny became more apparent. The process of creating music that was entirely hers, where she could express herself freely without compromise, was an essential part of her evolution as an artist. This realization led Sophie to become more involved in the production of her music, ultimately gaining the ability to craft a sound that was distinctly her own.

The transformation from a pop artist making music based on external influences to a fully autonomous artist was a significant milestone for Sophie. Her increasing control over her music came not only from a desire for creative independence but from a growing belief in her own ability to direct her artistic journey. With *Trip the Light Fantastic* (2007), Sophie began to take on a larger role in the album's production, marking a clear departure from the earlier days when her contributions were limited to vocal performance. This shift allowed her to refine her style and ensure that her work was a true reflection of her creative voice.

By taking charge of the production process, Sophie not only gained more freedom in her music but also began to experiment with new sounds, going beyond the catchy pop anthems that initially made her famous. She was able to explore different genres and production techniques, incorporating elements of electronic music, rock, and even a bit of soul. These creative decisions gave Sophie the opportunity to further explore her artistic range, making her music not only more personal but also more complex and layered. As a result, *Trip the Light Fantastic* struck a balance between mainstream pop appeal and deeper, more introspective content that demonstrated her growth as an artist.

However, this artistic freedom wasn't without its own challenges. As Sophie gained more control over her work, she also faced the pressure to maintain the success she had achieved with her earlier hits. The commercial demands of the music industry have a way of forcing artists into a particular mold, and Sophie was no different. She knew that her early success was due in large part to her ability to produce catchy, radio-friendly music. Yet, she also understood that in order to truly evolve, she had to resist the temptation to simply repeat the past.

This balance between creative freedom and the commercial pressures of the industry is something Sophie has navigated throughout her career. With each album, she has faced the challenge of staying true to her evolving sound while still delivering music that resonates with her audience. Sophie's growth as an artist has always involved a careful balancing act: how to remain authentic to her creative vision while also remaining relevant in the ever-changing landscape of pop music.

Throughout her career, Sophie's lyrics have reflected her own personal journey. Early on, her songs were often light-hearted, catchy, and focused on themes of love and fun. As she gained more creative control, however, Sophie began to explore deeper, more personal themes. This shift in her songwriting was a natural evolution as she grew older and experienced more of life's complexities. The lyrics of her later albums, especially *Familia* (2016), reflect a more mature, introspective perspective, where Sophie addressed her experiences as a woman, a mother, and an artist. Her willingness to embrace vulnerability and explore these more intimate themes allowed her to connect with her audience on a much deeper level.

One of the most significant aspects of Sophie's growth as an artist has been her ability to tackle the balance between her public persona and her private life. In a world where public figures are often scrutinized for every detail of their personal lives, Sophie has always been mindful of this divide. She has spoken candidly about how fame can sometimes feel like a double-edged sword, with the desire to remain authentic sometimes clashing with the pressure to maintain a polished public image. Over the years, Sophie has found a way to navigate this balance, using her music to speak about the challenges and joys of her life without oversharing or feeling the need to meet the expectations of the media.

This journey toward personal growth has allowed Sophie to stay true to herself as an artist. She has resisted the temptation to conform to the ever-shifting standards of the music industry, and instead, has focused on creating music that feels honest and true to her. Her ability to write songs that speak to universal themes while also reflecting her personal experiences has been one of the key factors in her longevity as an artist. Sophie's music is not just about catchy hooks or radio hits; it's about creating a genuine connection with her audience, something that goes beyond the superficial aspects of fame.

As Sophie continued to take control over her music, she also took on greater responsibility for the production of her albums. This shift in her creative process gave her the freedom to experiment with different musical styles, collaborate with new producers, and explore a broader range of emotions and themes. Her later albums, such as *Make a Scene* (2011), showcase her ability to adapt to changing musical trends while still remaining true to her artistic roots. *Make a Scene* marked a bold departure from her earlier pop sound, incorporating elements of electronic dance music and reflecting the growing influence of EDM in the global music scene.

The shift toward electronic music was just one example of how Sophie's sound evolved over time. Rather than adhering to a formula that had worked in the past, she embraced the opportunity to explore new genres and sounds. This willingness to experiment with different styles of music is a key aspect of Sophie's career. She has never been afraid to step outside of her comfort zone, and this creative freedom has allowed her to stay relevant and maintain her authenticity as an artist.

Sophie's decision to take on more creative control also marked a significant shift in the way she approached her music videos and live performances. Early in her career, Sophie's visual style was often shaped by the trends of the time. However, as she became more involved in her music, she began to take a more hands-on approach to her visual identity as well. Sophie's music videos began to reflect her artistic vision, showcasing her personality and the themes she was exploring in her music. This shift in her visual identity was not just about aesthetics—it was about aligning her music with a deeper, more personal expression of who she was.

Through it all, Sophie's commitment to personal growth and creative freedom has remained unwavering. She has always been willing to take risks and push herself outside of her comfort zone, whether in her music, her lyrics, or her visual style. The journey of self-discovery that Sophie has undertaken over the years has allowed her to stay true to herself while evolving as an artist. She has continuously challenged herself to explore new sounds and themes while never losing sight of the authenticity that has made her so relatable to her audience.

In the years since her debut, Sophie Ellis-Bextor has transformed from a pop star into a deeply respected and influential artist. Her willingness to take control of her music and her creative direction has been instrumental in her growth as a musician. Sophie's evolution as an artist is not just about the changes in her sound; it's about the freedom she has found in expressing herself on her own terms. By embracing her personal growth and using her platform to explore deeper themes, Sophie has crafted a body of work that resonates with her audience and continues to inspire.

Chapter 7

Facing Challenges and Finding New Paths

Sophie Ellis-Bextor's journey through the music industry has not been without its hurdles, but it is precisely these challenges that have defined her growth as an artist. From the early pressures of fame to the more personal struggles she faced later in her career, Sophie's story is one of resilience and determination. This chapter reflects on the challenges that Sophie has encountered, both professionally and personally, and how she overcame them by staying true to herself and her music. Despite the obstacles she faced, Sophie managed to find new paths forward, always evolving and embracing the opportunities for growth that life presented.

In the beginning, when Sophie transitioned from *Theaudience* to a solo career, the shift was not easy. The early success of her debut album *Read My Lips* (2001) brought Sophie into the limelight, but with this fame came an entirely new set of challenges. The pressure to replicate the commercial success of her first album was immense, and Sophie quickly learned that being a solo artist meant having the spotlight firmly placed on her. For someone who had been used to working as part of a group, the weight of being the only focus of attention was both exhilarating and overwhelming. The industry, the fans, and even the media now had heightened expectations for her to deliver hit after hit, a demand that could easily become suffocating for any artist.

Despite these pressures, Sophie began to realize that success in the music industry is fleeting and often defined by commercial achievements. While she certainly enjoyed the recognition her music received, she found herself longing for more creative freedom. Sophie wanted to explore new sounds and ideas without being constrained by the need to fit into the mold of a mainstream pop star. This realization led to a shift in her approach to music, as she started to take more control over the direction of her work. This period of self-reflection allowed Sophie to gain confidence in her artistic choices, even when those choices didn't always align with industry expectations.

As Sophie began working on her second album, *Shoot from the Hip* (2003), she moved away from the pure dance-pop sound of her debut and sought out a more experimental approach. The album incorporated influences from rock, jazz, and soul, pushing Sophie into new territory. The risk was evident—many fans and critics expected her to replicate the success of her first album, but Sophie refused to be confined to that path. She was determined to explore the full spectrum of her creativity, even if it meant facing the uncertainty of a mixed reception. *Shoot from the Hip* received both praise and criticism. Some listeners admired her willingness to experiment, while others felt that the album lacked the catchy, radio-friendly hits that had made her a household name.

The mixed response from critics and fans could have been discouraging for any artist, but Sophie chose to use it as an opportunity for growth. The experience taught her that not every creative risk would result in immediate success, but that didn't mean she should shy away from taking them. The most important lesson was that staying true to her artistic vision was more fulfilling than simply chasing after the next hit song. The feedback from *Shoot from the Hip* only reinforced her commitment to following her instincts and evolving as an artist, even if that meant stepping away from what had worked in the past.

Along with her creative challenges, Sophie's personal life began to play a more significant role in her music. The pressures of balancing a high-profile career with a personal life were not lost on her, and as she matured, Sophie found herself more reflective in her songwriting. As a public figure, Sophie was constantly in the spotlight, but she began to feel the weight of trying to maintain a private life while her every move was scrutinized. She was no longer just an artist with a catchy pop tune; she was a person with real emotions, relationships, and experiences, and she began to channel these aspects into her work. Sophie's music became more personal and introspective, touching on themes of love, identity, and motherhood.

Her third album, *Trip the Light Fantastic* (2007), marked a return to a more radio-friendly sound but still retained the depth and complexity that had begun to characterize Sophie's work. It was clear that while Sophie was still interested in creating pop music, she was also interested in exploring more layered, emotional themes in her lyrics. The success of "Catch You" demonstrated that Sophie could strike a balance between maintaining her commercial appeal and staying true to her creative self. *Trip the Light Fantastic* was a defining moment in Sophie's career, as it proved that she could adapt to the changing music industry while still holding onto the authenticity that made her unique.

As Sophie continued to evolve, she faced yet another challenge: how to remain relevant in an industry that constantly shifts and changes. The rise of electronic dance music, changing listener preferences, and a growing emphasis on social media and personal branding created new demands for artists. Sophie embraced these changes, using them to fuel her creativity rather than letting them limit her. She started collaborating with different producers and experimenting with new genres. Her 2011 album *Make a Scene* marked a departure from her previous work, embracing a more electronic, dance-driven sound. It was clear that Sophie was no longer interested in simply being a pop star in the traditional sense; she was an artist willing to embrace the modern landscape of music and experiment with new styles.

Make a Scene was a bold move, and it didn't achieve the same level of commercial success as some of her earlier albums. However, it was a critical moment in Sophie's career, as it showed that she was unafraid to challenge herself and reinvent her sound. The album's collaboration with several renowned DJs and producers in the EDM scene allowed Sophie to step outside the realm of traditional pop and into the world of electronic music. While *Make a Scene* was a departure from her earlier work, it was still a reflection of Sophie's ongoing journey as an artist, one that had been shaped by her desire for creative freedom and her willingness to take risks.

Through all these creative shifts, Sophie faced personal challenges as well. The experience of being a mother, managing the responsibilities of family life, and maintaining a public career presented its own set of difficulties. Sophie often spoke about the struggle to balance her career with her role as a mother, and how these two aspects of her life could sometimes clash. The demands of the music industry, with its constant travel, media obligations, and the pressure to maintain a certain image, sometimes made it difficult for Sophie to find time for herself and her family. Yet, it was in these moments of personal reflection and growth that Sophie found a new source of inspiration. Her experiences as a mother, navigating the complexities of love, family, and identity, began to seep into her music, giving it a deeper, more introspective quality.

Sophie's willingness to be open about the challenges she faced in both her personal and professional life allowed her to connect with her audience in a more authentic way. She used her platform to speak about motherhood, relationships, and personal growth, offering her fans a window into her life. This honesty and vulnerability became a defining feature of Sophie's music, setting her apart from many of her contemporaries who preferred to keep their personal lives private.

By embracing her struggles and using them as creative fuel, Sophie was able to grow not only as an artist but as a person. The challenges she faced in her career—whether dealing with the pressures of fame, the evolving nature of the music industry, or balancing her personal life with her public persona—shaped her as an artist in ways that were both profound and empowering. Sophie's ability to push through difficult times and find new paths forward is a powerful part of her story. It is a reminder that growth and reinvention are not just about musical experimentation but about overcoming life's obstacles and continuing to create in the face of adversity.

Chapter 8

Behind the Scenes – Sophie Ellis-Bextor's Personal Life

Sophie's relationship with her family has been one of the most significant sources of strength throughout her career. Married to Richard Jones, the bassist for *The Feeling*, Sophie has built a life grounded in mutual respect and shared experiences. Their partnership has been a constant in her life, offering Sophie a sense of stability amid the often-chaotic world of fame and public scrutiny. Sophie has described her marriage as a pillar that supports her both personally and professionally. In an industry that often puts artists at the center of attention, Sophie's relationship with Richard has allowed her to maintain a sense of normalcy, providing a sanctuary where she can be herself away from the limelight.

Their marriage has not only been a source of emotional support but also a partnership that enriches both of their creative lives. Richard, being a musician himself, understands the demands of the music industry, which has allowed them to navigate their professional lives with mutual understanding. Sophie has often spoken about the joy of having a partner who is not only a supportive figure but also someone who shares a common understanding of the challenges that come with their work. Their shared experiences in the music industry have helped them build a relationship based on empathy, trust, and a deep connection.

Motherhood has also been a transformative part of Sophie's personal journey, profoundly influencing both her life and her music. When Sophie became a mother, it brought a new dimension to her understanding of the world. The birth of her children opened up a wealth of new emotions and experiences that Sophie channeled into her music. Her role as a mother has influenced many of the themes in her songs, particularly those that explore love, family, and identity. Sophie's ability to express her experiences as a mother through her music has added a layer of depth to her work, allowing her to connect with her audience in a more meaningful and relatable way.

While Sophie has always been dedicated to her music, becoming a mother prompted her to reassess how she approached her career. The demands of raising children while maintaining a successful career in the public eye are not easy to balance. Sophie has been candid about the challenges of trying to juggle these responsibilities. At times, it has meant making sacrifices in her career, whether it was taking time away from touring or limiting her availability for public appearances. Yet, Sophie has always been clear that her family comes first, and her children have become her central source of inspiration. Her journey as a mother has allowed her to develop a deeper understanding of herself and her work, adding authenticity and emotional depth to her music.

Balancing the demands of a high-profile career and personal life has never been straightforward. Sophie has spoken openly about the complexities of being a mother and an artist. The pressures of maintaining a career while also ensuring her family life remains intact are challenges that many artists face, and Sophie is no exception. Yet, despite these pressures, she has found ways to make both parts of her life coexist. Sophie has learned to prioritize her family without neglecting her artistic ambitions. This balance is not always easy, but it has allowed her to remain grounded in her personal life while continuing to build her career.

One of the significant aspects of Sophie's personal life is how she has managed to maintain a sense of privacy despite her fame. In an era where celebrities often share every aspect of their lives on social media, Sophie has kept much of her family life private. She has been intentional about keeping certain parts of her personal world separate from the public's view, allowing her to maintain a sense of normalcy. Sophie's ability to keep her home life private while still engaging with her fans in a meaningful way speaks to her desire to retain a sense of individuality beyond her public persona.

Sophie's decision to share aspects of her life with her audience, particularly through social media and interviews, has allowed her fans to connect with her on a deeper level. Her openness about motherhood, her relationship with Richard, and the everyday joys and challenges of life has made Sophie a more relatable figure to her audience. Her authenticity resonates with fans, who appreciate her willingness to share her personal journey in a way that feels genuine and unpretentious. Sophie has always strived to be true to herself, both in her music and in her personal life, and this transparency has built a strong bond with her followers.

Sophie's connection to her fans goes beyond the surface level of her music. She has shared her experiences as a mother, her struggles with balancing career and family, and her thoughts on the complexities of life as a public figure. This openness allows her to be more than just a pop star; it makes her someone who can relate to her audience's experiences. Sophie's ability to open up and share her story has made her an artist that fans not only admire but also feel connected to on a personal level.

Despite the challenges that come with being in the public eye, Sophie has managed to preserve her sense of self and protect her family life. She has always been conscious of the fine line between her professional and personal worlds, making an effort to maintain boundaries while still being open and engaging with her fans. Sophie's ability to balance these competing demands speaks to her strength of character and her commitment to her family. Her willingness to share certain aspects of her life, while maintaining privacy where necessary, reflects her deep sense of responsibility to both her fans and her loved ones.

Throughout her career, Sophie has stayed true to the values that matter most to her—her family, her authenticity, and her creative vision. These values have shaped both her music and her approach to life. Sophie's personal life has allowed her to explore deeper themes in her music; from the love she feels for her family to the emotional depth of her own experiences. Her role as a wife and mother has provided a foundation of stability that has helped her maintain focus on her music, while also keeping her grounded in the realities of everyday life.

Chapter 9

Perimenopop – The Creative Spark Behind Her Latest Work

As Sophie enters a new chapter, both in her personal life and her career, *Perimenopop* stands as a celebration of the transformations she's going through. The title itself, with its clever wordplay, hints at the age-related transitions many women experiences, particularly perimenopause, but Sophie uses this phase to speak more broadly about the changes that come with growing older. The album goes beyond one specific experience—it's about embracing the inevitability of change, empowering oneself through it, and finding new forms of strength and creativity. Sophie uses *Perimenopop* to explore these themes with a sense of humor, grace, and depth, making it a personal, yet universally relatable, record.

Sophie Ellis-Bextor

The creative spark behind *Perimenopop* was fueled by Sophie's growing desire to create something that truly represented where she was in her life—emotionally and artistically. Unlike earlier projects, where she may have felt more inclined to cater to commercial expectations or the pressures of the music industry, this time Sophie was driven by a need to make music that felt authentic to her current experiences. This album marks a shift in Sophie's relationship with her work, moving from the desire to make hits to a deeper wish to express herself fully, drawing from her personal life and evolving perspective.

The process of creating *Perimenopop* was deeply introspective. Sophie worked with several collaborators, each bringing something new to the table, but she remained very much at the helm of the creative direction. The shift towards a more hands-on approach was reflective of her desire to own her music fully, to be not just the performer but the architect of her sound. Sophie had a clear vision for the album, wanting it to capture the energy of a woman fully embracing change, not running from it. The production features a mixture of electronic beats, pop elements, and sophisticated arrangements, but it all serves a bigger purpose—serving as the soundtrack to Sophie's journey through self-empowerment and the strength to move through life's transitions.

One of the most defining aspects of *Perimenopop* is its exploration of empowerment. Sophie has always been an advocate for expressing personal strength through music, and this album is no different. What makes it unique, though, is the rawness and honesty with which she addresses themes of transformation and self-discovery. *Perimenopop* is not just about the joy of embracing change but about taking ownership of it, finding your own voice through the noise of external expectations. The music doesn't shy away from the complexities of change—whether it's physical, emotional, or creative—but it also celebrates the beauty in the process of reinvention.

Resilience is another key theme in the album. Sophie's journey to this point has not always been smooth. She's faced the challenges of maintaining relevance in a rapidly changing music industry, the struggles of balancing her personal life with her career, and the natural human ups and downs that come with aging. Rather than letting these challenges stop her, Sophie has used them to fuel her creativity. She channels these experiences into her music, making each track feel like a step toward overcoming obstacles and embracing new possibilities. The album serves as a reminder that resilience is not just about enduring hardships—it's about finding new ways to move forward, with strength and optimism.

The theme of embracing change runs throughout *Perimenopop*. Sophie's reflections on age and experience are woven into the fabric of the album, but it's more about embracing the next phase of life with open arms, knowing that change is inevitable but also an opportunity for growth. This attitude comes through clearly in the music, which feels like a fresh take on her sound, while still retaining the elements that made Sophie's music unique in the first place. There's a sense of openness to experimentation in the album, a willingness to explore new sounds and styles while staying true to her roots.

For Sophie, creating *Perimenopop* wasn't just about producing a collection of songs—it was about telling a story. The album reflects her growth as an artist and as a person. As she approaches the next stage of her life, Sophie wanted to create something that felt like a natural reflection of where she was emotionally, both as a woman and an artist. Each track on the album speaks to a different facet of this experience, whether it's confronting personal doubts, celebrating newfound strength, or embracing the challenges of change. The album is Sophie's way of sharing her journey, and in doing so, it allows her to connect with her listeners on a much deeper level.

The songwriting on *Perimenopop* is perhaps some of Sophie's most personal work to date. The lyrics explore vulnerability, self-reflection, and the internal dialogue that comes with navigating life's transitions. Sophie has always been known for her ability to write catchy pop songs, but this time, there's an added layer of emotional depth. The themes of self-empowerment, strength, and resilience resonate strongly throughout the album, not only in the music but in the way Sophie shares her personal experiences. The songs invite listeners into Sophie's world, offering a glimpse of her emotional journey while also encouraging them to reflect on their own experiences.

Musically, *Perimenopop* blends different influences, drawing from electronic pop, disco, and even indie elements. The album doesn't adhere to one specific genre but rather combines different styles that feel true to Sophie's evolving sound. The production is fresh, with a modern, yet timeless, quality that aligns with Sophie's desire to explore new musical territory. The album moves between upbeat, danceable tracks and more reflective, introspective moments, creating a balanced listening experience. It's a dynamic record, one that's filled with energy but also carries moments of quiet vulnerability.

In terms of collaboration, Sophie worked with a number of talented producers and songwriters who brought their unique perspectives to the project. These collaborations were key to helping Sophie push the boundaries of her sound while maintaining her distinct voice. However, it's clear that Sophie remains the driving force behind the album. She has taken a more active role in shaping the final product, ensuring that *Perimenopop* is not just the result of a collaborative process but a personal statement that reflects her journey and her artistic vision.

The evolution of Sophie's sound over the years has been marked by a willingness to embrace new ideas while staying rooted in her core musical identity. *Perimenopop* is no exception to this, but it represents a more complete picture of Sophie as an artist. It's a reflection of her growth—not just in terms of her musical ability, but in how she views herself and the world around her. This new album captures a sense of freedom and empowerment that Sophie feels as she moves forward, fully embracing the changes that life has to offer.

Sophie's journey with *Perimenopop* is a celebration of both the challenges and joys that come with embracing new phases of life. It is a testament to the idea that reinvention is not just about making new music—it's about growing and evolving as a person and allowing that growth to be reflected in your art. Sophie has always been an artist who doesn't shy away from change, and with *Perimenopop*, she has embraced it fully. The album represents her ability to adapt, experiment, and stay true to herself, while also finding new ways to express her personal and creative vision.

Chapter 10

Looking Ahead – Sophie's Legacy and Continuing Impact

Sophie's career has always been marked by her ability to stay true to herself while adapting to the changing tides of the music industry. Her early success, propelled by *Read My Lips*, gave Sophie the platform to showcase her distinct pop sound—catchy, infectious, and full of energy. Tracks like "Groovejet (If This Ain't Love)" and "Murder on the Dancefloor" solidified her place in the music world, but even then, Sophie's unique artistry was evident. Unlike many pop stars of the early 2000s, Sophie refused to remain confined to a single genre or sound. As she transitioned from one album to the next, she embraced creative challenges, always seeking to grow, evolve, and stretch beyond her comfort zone.

Sophie Ellis-Bextor

The combination of her pop success and her willingness to take creative risks has been key to Sophie's staying power in a music industry that is known for its quick turnover. While many artists are known for one style or period, Sophie's ability to create fresh, relevant music while still maintaining her unique voice is a hallmark of her career. She has evolved as an artist in a way that has felt natural and deliberate, rather than trying to chase trends or rely on past formulas. Over the years, her music has reflected not only her growth as an artist but also her journey through life itself—one that has included moments of doubt, self-reflection, and empowerment.

Sophie's impact on pop music is not just confined to her own work, though. Her journey has been an inspiration to many, particularly for artists who want to explore more nuanced, complex forms of pop music. Sophie has always demonstrated that it's possible to be both commercially successful and creatively free. Her ability to make music that resonates with listeners on a deep level while remaining relevant in the fast-paced world of pop has been a significant influence on newer generations of artists. Whether they are drawn to her ability to blend pop with dance, indie, or even electronic music, many musicians today look to Sophie as an example of what it means to balance artistic integrity with the demands of the music industry.

Her impact goes beyond just the influence on other musicians. Sophie has inspired her fans with her authenticity, and this connection has been key to the loyalty of her fan base. While some artists keep their personal lives tightly guarded, Sophie has never shied away from sharing her experiences with her audience. From her candid reflections on motherhood to her insights about her own personal growth, Sophie has built a relationship with her fans that is based on trust and vulnerability. This emotional connection has allowed her to cultivate a fan base that is not just interested in her music but in her as a person. She remains grounded in her personal life, even as she continues to experience professional success, and this balance between her public and private selves is part of what makes her so relatable.

Sophie's approach to her music career has also shown that it's possible to evolve and grow in an industry that is often quick to discard older artists in favor of new, younger faces. While many of her peers in the pop world have faced the challenge of staying relevant, Sophie has managed to do so by continually pushing herself to try new things, experiment with different sounds, and remain true to her artistic vision. Her willingness to embrace change—whether it's in her music, her personal life, or how she interacts with her audience—has ensured that Sophie remains a force in the music world.

At the heart of Sophie's legacy is her authenticity. She has never tried to fit a mold or adhere to industry expectations that didn't align with her own values. Her music is deeply personal, and she has always used it as a platform to express her thoughts, emotions, and experiences. This authenticity has allowed her to build a connection with her audience that is far beyond the superficiality of typical pop stardom. Sophie's work is a reflection of her journey through life, and this transparency has made her music relatable and powerful for so many listeners.

In her most recent project, *Perimenopop*, Sophie continues to redefine herself as an artist. The album reflects her evolving journey as she navigates the changes that come with age, experience, and personal growth. The title, with its clever reference to perimenopause, speaks to the broader theme of embracing life's transitions—finding empowerment in moments of change, and using these experiences to fuel creative energy. The album touches on themes of resilience, self-discovery, and embracing new chapters, all of which resonate not just with Sophie's fans but with anyone who has faced their own transformative life moments.

Perimenopop is another example of Sophie's commitment to reinventing her sound while still remaining true to herself. The album blends elements of pop, dance, and electronic music, reflecting her continued exploration of new genres and sounds. It also brings a sense of empowerment and confidence, with Sophie's lyrics exploring personal strength, resilience, and the joy of embracing life's inevitable changes. As Sophie continues to grow as an artist and a person, *Perimenopop* captures that journey in a way that is both uplifting and reflective.

Looking ahead, it's clear that Sophie's legacy will continue to evolve, just as her music has. The future holds endless possibilities for Sophie as an artist, as she has proven time and time again that she is not afraid to take creative risks. What makes her journey so inspiring is her ability to push past the boundaries that are often imposed by the industry and create music that is authentic to her experiences. Sophie has shown that it is possible to evolve while staying true to who you are, and this is a powerful lesson for aspiring artists everywhere.

Sophie's legacy, however, is not just about the music she has created. It is about the way she has approached her career—how she has balanced her personal life with her professional obligations, how she has remained grounded despite the pressures of fame, and how she has stayed true to her artistic vision. Her ability to connect with her audience, be vulnerable in her music, and experiment with new sounds is what has kept her relevant, even after all these years. Sophie has built a lasting legacy that goes beyond commercial success—she has created a body of work that speaks to her growth, her authenticity, and her unwavering commitment to her craft.

Looking forward, there is no doubt that Sophie Ellis-Bextor's story is far from finished. With each new project, she continues to reinvent herself, embracing new phases of life and new challenges. She shows no signs of slowing down and remains as passionate about her music as ever. The future is full of exciting possibilities for Sophie, and her fans eagerly await what comes next. Her impact on the music world is undeniable, and as she continues to create, inspire, and evolve, her legacy will continue to grow.

Epilogue

As we wrap up this exploration of Sophie Ellis-Bextor's life and career, I want to extend a heartfelt thank you to you for choosing to join me on this journey. Whether you've been a long-time fan of Sophie's music or you're just discovering her work, I hope this book has offered a fresh perspective on her artistry and the remarkable story behind it. Sophie's journey is more than just one of musical success—it's a story of personal growth, resilience, and the ongoing pursuit of creative freedom.

Throughout this book, we've seen how Sophie's music has evolved, how her personal experiences have shaped her artistry, and how she has navigated the complexities of fame, motherhood, and self-discovery. Each phase of Sophie's career has added a new layer to her legacy, and it's clear that her ability to reinvent herself, while staying true to her core values, is what has allowed her to remain relevant and influential in an ever-changing industry.

Sophie's story reminds us all that being an artist is not about staying stagnant but about embracing change, taking risks, and finding new ways to express ourselves as we grow.

Sophie's impact on the music world is undeniable. From her early hits that defined the pop landscape of the early 2000s to her more introspective and experimental work in recent years, Sophie has continuously pushed the boundaries of what pop music can be. She has inspired countless artists to take creative risks, embrace authenticity, and evolve with time. Her music has provided comfort, joy, and inspiration to many, offering both uplifting anthems and deeply personal reflections. Sophie has shown that music has the power to connect us, to reflect our own experiences, and to help us navigate the complexities of life.

But beyond the music, it is Sophie's resilience, her ability to stay grounded, and her openness to change that have shaped her legacy. In a world where the music industry is often quick to discard older artists, Sophie has proven that there is always room to evolve and redefine one's career. She has taught us that growing older does not mean fading into the background—it means embracing new opportunities, continuing to create, and using life's transitions to fuel our creativity. Sophie's journey is not just about her success in the spotlight, but also about the strength and determination it takes to continue moving forward, even when faced with challenges.

As we look ahead, there is no doubt that Sophie's legacy will continue to evolve. The music she creates, the stories she shares, and the authenticity she brings to her work will ensure that her influence extends far beyond the present moment. With each new project, Sophie reinvents herself, keeping her sound fresh and exciting while staying connected to the experiences that matter most. And while the future is always uncertain, one thing is clear: Sophie's artistic journey is far from over.

Sophie Ellis-Bexton

Sophie's ability to remain relevant in an ever-changing industry speaks volumes about her dedication to her craft and her commitment to staying true to herself. She has shown us that success in the music world is not just about following trends or chasing the next hit—it's about creating music that is meaningful and personal, music that reflects who you are and where you are in life. Sophie's work is a reflection of her journey, and her willingness to evolve and grow as an artist is something we can all learn from.

As you close this book, I hope you carry with you the insights and inspiration that Sophie's story offers. Her journey is a reminder that we are all capable of reinventing ourselves, of embracing change, and of finding strength in the face of life's challenges. Sophie's legacy is not just about the music she's created, but about the lessons she's imparted through her work: the importance of authenticity, the power of self-expression, and the strength that comes from embracing change with open arms.

Your own journey, just like Sophie's, is shaped by the experiences you encounter and the choices you make. Whether you are an artist, a creator, or simply someone navigating life's twists and turns, Sophie's story encourages us all to keep evolving, to find our voice, and to use our experiences to fuel our creativity.

Thank you once again for reading and for taking the time to explore Sophie's life and work. If you found this book valuable or have thoughts to share, I would truly appreciate your feedback. Your opinion matters! Please consider leaving an honest review on Amazon, as your thoughts help me improve future editions of this book and ensure that others can find the information they need. I look forward to hearing your perspective, and I hope this book has inspired you in the same way that Sophie's music continues to inspire so many.

As we reflect on Sophie's ongoing journey, there is a sense of anticipation for what comes next. Sophie has shown that no matter where we are in life, there is always room to grow, explore new avenues, and continue creating. With every album, every performance, and every new chapter, Sophie reminds us that the power of music and the courage to evolve will always lead to new and exciting paths. The future is bright, and Sophie's story is far from finished. Thank you for being part of her journey, and for taking the time to reflect on the music, the stories, and the messages that continue to resonate with so many.

Printed in Dunstable, United Kingdom